PEACE IN EXILE

Poems by David Oates

Oyster River Press

Cover art by Joan Darlington
Photo by Christiane Covington

Acknowledgements:

Many of these poems first appeared in
*Bitterroot,   Galley Sail,   Green Fuse,
Poetry/LA, Proof Rock and Wide Open*

Other books from the Oyster River Press:

*A Letter to my Daughter, 1687 by the Marquis of
Halifax* with *Essays from a New England College
Town (1927-1987)* by Phoebe Taylor.   2nd Ed.
1992.   ISBN 0 9617481 4 1
*The Mending of the Sky and other Chinese
Myths* Retold by Xiao Ming Li . Illustrations from
Shan Ming Wu. 1989.   ISBN 0 9617481 3 3
Thoughts for the Free Life. Lao Tsu to the Present.
2nd ed. 1989. Phoebe Taylor, Ed. Illustrated.
ISBN 0 9617481 5 X
*Ombres et Soleil / Sun and Shadows. Poems and
writings by Paul Eluard.* Translations C. Buckley
& Lloyd Alexander. 1992. Illus. Picasso, Magritte,
Man Ray, Chagall. ISBN 0 9617481 7 6
*Intense Experience. Social Psychology through
Poetry.* Frederick Samuels, PhD, Ed. 1990
ISBN 0 9617481 6 8

O y s t e r   R i v e r   P r e s s
20 Riverview Road   Durham   NH 03824

Dedication

To the loyal patrons of Galapagos Saloon: Ken W., Vickie and Al, Mary, Linda W., Ken and Sandy, Keith and Colleen, Joseph, Bobbi, Cathleen, John, and Kathy

CONTENTS

I. Chaparral

II. Kern

III. Mountain

IV. Desert

V. Edge

VI. Lo-ku

I. CHAPARRAL

EVEN HERE

The roar of images and sounds impounds us
like ancient city walls — keeping out the world,
keeping in beloved mayhem, barter,
smells, deceit and favor. Nothing astounds us
but news: politicians, boy versus girl,
anything pungent enough and rank. No heart or
discovery of quiet need intrude.
This is the city: Get. Consume. Feud.

Yet someone, rooftop, carries water for her son
whose vine of melons steeps in warmth, half-grown.
Rains on distant soils soak deep and run
toward the city. The good does its work unknown.
Even here, it is love that grounds us.
Even here, where Babylon surrounds us.

PEACE IN EXILE

peace in exile
I am always finding

and exile in the midst of peace

the softest kiss brings teeth to bare
and eating's embrace drips blood from the chin

beyond the dearness of love
flesh unto flesh and bone

no illusion is not blown through at last
by wind of reality

bulldozer cyclone
temporary as a thought

no home was ever kept
except in lying lavender of memory

and yet no awful berth cannot make sleep for a night
lost in wild or far too found behind the barbs

and in waking to the body the light spun down
upon the planet's edge
the breath

find sweet what is
and will never be again

INTO THE VALLEY

I. *Where he stands*

Grandpa
drives into the Valley orchards to tend bees

hands like a stevedore
cupping the bees gently, two palmed,
opening to them a rough flesh flower they like
crawling in and out innocently
while he watches.

By the Ventura road there's a tavern or two.
Fresh Glendale puts up low-browed bungalows
grows hydrangea bushes in front
hopes for Mediterraneans and terra cotta roofs.
Dark long-barred saloons serve Grandpa their nickel
beers
with bowls of white eggs beneath the high ceilings
and slow fans circling, with pretzels and walnuts and
all
he had lived on once, years ago, getting started

but that is past and now
a couple great years before the Great War
randy as a cock and banty in his sheet-metal arms
lean-butted Bill comes in for a beer and
if it's Friday night, for knocking fists.

His dense farm-labored bones crack against all comers.
I think he wins, always I think he was winning
(until the second one up, the ring-knuckle
pushed back into his hand, stayed there
till he showed me
tough grey hairs and age spots on the big hands

and the one knuckle, the one counting March
in that days-in-the-month trick I never learned,
still drew back, stubbornly, to insist
there was more to Grandpa than his white lion-mane
his good suits and careful manners)
and if he feels like it he picks a fight
just for the hell.

Grandpa wears large-armed white shirts, collarless
and suspendered, out into the groves to tend bees:
the heavy drone sweating through the orange leaves
and a slice of summer brilliance gilding fine dust
that sifts and settles on his brown shoe toes
and on the ripe globed fruits suspended around him
like the numerous planets of a foolish, wealthy sun

until at last he stands
one arm raised to wipe the brow
and a snap-billed cap held high.
The steamer waits off aways
dusty and chipped but bravely red
the sweet water-smell of irrigation mud
rises around him in this hot land
this droning paradise

and there he stands, regardful of honey
potent as oranges
still as the earth.

o o o

I know where he stood like that:
now it's Sepulveda Boulevard, almost Roscoe,
near the Winchell's Donuts.

6

Sometimes I know what's under those streets
as if I lifted them up and looked
or didn't need to: as if
I lived right through them
into the Valley.

Sometimes I feel under the sidewalk
careful, dark, and slow
buckle it up with my mind
like slowest treeroots
like muscle tightening beneath
to draw and press back the broken slabs

for sumac to arise
for woodlitter and brushy scrub to breathe
for dead earth to know live dust again
and feel the tickle of a centipede track
traced across the tender and potential plain.

II. *Forever*

When it's hot in LA it's murder in the Valley.
The sweat on your back collects grime out of the air
and grits up beneath your T-shirt until you stink.
When you drive out by the airport
along Foothill beneath the powerlines
they sound like the place looks
a high fretful buzz
that makes the back of your eyes ache.
Hot light diffracts across the stagnant sky
as if we'd made our home in an arc lamp
and kept the juice turned up
just to show we could.

Grandpa rode the train to get here
long back almost to the 'oughts
and walked beneath a clear sun to somewhere
for work. For a time he was fourteen, solo,
scared, scrambling. Then one by one
he brought mother, sisters out from
widow-Indian Okie squalor. He did his part
to get and have and marry
worked in what was becoming Glendale
saw a chance on Sunset and built there
got a Court out on that Ventura road.
He did better what everyone tried doing
covered and crossed and owned up the earth
had his own house tiled and Spanish-porched and
shadowed from the sun.

He found a girl who rode the yellow streetcars
and sang in churches cool and rosy
as if the touch of her hand belonged there
and in the big dark churchy theaters
where he followed her later
to get a kiss
put his arms around
steal her away for good.

By and by
he put his boys under movie-wide cowboy hats
placed them on horses out in the golden fields
of North Hollywood, where they rode
between the sole oaks and summergrass
and watered their mounts in
of all things
the actual LA river

and all of them
must have been unconscious
the boys, the rosy girl, the kin
drowsing in the earth and sun of it
living a land so real
they never thought to keep it
never thought to notice, never thought
it wouldn't hold them
like gravity
like the arms of a lover
never thought it wouldn't hold them like Grandpa held
them
tight and hard, forever.

III.   *Memory map*

What is this place?
The boulevard heads west
as true as any explorer's heart
seeking the hem of the garment of pure yearning
as straight as the eyeshot of the desert traveller
sensing the invisible mark
that promises deliverance to cool horizons
out of the sunblasted reptile-breeding maze

as true, as straight, as faithless and pocked
as any diseased outcast
casually knifing his way west.
That's my street
laid out winsomely geometric
then gang-raped by every
real-estate lackey in town.
A whore of a street who
followed the bands of drifters west
who gave up, set down, opened shop
right here. My home.

Opened a hill with a knife.
Opened her eyes to the possibilities.
Opened chaparral
and found weedlots.

Opened Used Cars beside them. Opened
a spew of liquor stores, opened
her legs to acres of apartments
stacked in pink stucco the same in all directions
without a slope or a green leaf
to forgive the sun by
not a shred of a place to hide in
not a place at all

but some kind of sleepwalking TV dream
a crippled contentment of stunned consumers
invented by this very street, right here
my home. My boulevard.

o   o   o

What is this place?
When did I wake up here? When
did my fathers lay me down tenderly
in the remembered nights of cool hillsides
and sing, even — sing! — out of the trusting dark
stroking my forehead and looking off
or in?

I know this, too,
not as I know the ill-dreamt boulevard
but like an inherited memory
a sense I cannot explain
unshakable, precise, unlikely
that blesses in waking and in sleep.

10

I know that where I grew up
there were blackberries in rows to prick your hands
and to leave red stains and to discover.
There were hillslopes above
alien smogs that seldom overtook us
for we were busy and safe to explore
among the chaparral, we were dust covered and wily
like keen-eyed coyotes — so we thought —
unafraid of low paths beneath the scrub
that ran you to little brush warrens,
round secrets held amidst the thorny ocean
of buck brush and ceanothus and sumac
where we sat crosslegged and broke the hollow twigs
strewn by pasts and seasons we never thought about
never understanding that none would replace them.

Coyotes, brush, blackberries, snap twigs,
the whole thriving life
we scarcely imagined, save in blundering moments:
that fox, the rabbits we'd surprise, the
mysterious birds always present just out of sight
threading their purposes low and rustling
among the canebrake and flickered light
and most of all that unimaginable buck
standing motionless on our drive
waiting for me to round the corner home from school
waiting to deliver that moment into my hands forever
to speak across the asphalt in eyes
then vanish —
this whole thriving life we never knew
except as rootstems know the curve
of stones rugged or smooth
grasped far below.

We were in our fathers' land, and
knew the sun's rising would be bright in summer
dim-bright and moist other times,
would lead along paths between the wide spaced
casual streets, downhill along backs of houses and
            wheelbarrows
and faraway chicken coops, whitefeathered and always
stirring,
which sent such morning sounds across the acres and
            windowsills
as made the boys rise early
and find the mother poised and still
coffee half-cooled beside the red-edged bible
laid flat on the breakfast table while
she followed the distant arcs of birds
against the far Verdugos
and we stood rubbing sleep from our eyes
silently.

o   o   o

This was the land of old dreams
rock-walled and planted and pipe-laid
and abandoned. Old grape vines
and fruit trees, walnut and apricot and fig
left by nameless improvidents
whose fertile foolishness just touched the land
so that our coming seemed a readiness, a return
a promise kept.

In the middle of a wildness would shine
an aged white sapling
canopied and vined into permanent adolescence
hardy and fruitless
charmed by the ghostly hint of an earthen ring.

12

Then others would appear pale and useless
still straight in the nether light
beneath the chaparral
and carven-handled spigots would sprout
over secret systems of red-rusted waterpipes
fabulous as lost jewel-eyed buddhas to us
forgotten beneath vertical yards of brush
signs of our fathers left there for us
to imagine.

We may have heard of old ranches, Mexican names,
landgrants. We saw wild vines still bearing
abundant, beyond remembering
departed harvesters, planters, bringers of water.

All this was ours, ours from forebringers wild and
unnamed
come strangely to wonder
as we did.
All this was ours.

No premonition forescared us
that would be squashed, obliterated
by a tract as wide as horizons
unrolled like linoleum
across it all.

IV.   *Creosote and yerba buena*

Double seeing aches my eyes when
I try to cross the Valley.
Too often I lose the thread, wander
catching the bitter whiff of creosote bush
mixed with yerba buena, sweet and sunny,
beneath the fumes of heavy traffic
like a trick, a false hope, an illusion.
Fear of knowing and remembering
teaches me to avoid that corner, that one spot
where sometimes yet a man stands motionless,
one arm raised to wipe the brow
and a snap-billed cap held high,
with the pleasure of work upon him —
not on the curb quite, not
looking at the Winchell's, not
hearing the music hammering
from rows of restless cars
waiting and going and waiting and going —

but listening, for a moment
to the buzz of bees rising
and to the sound, if there is one,
of sunlight on sand and leaf and skin

and then I wonder that he does not hear
the roar of choices and chances
his sons of sons and sons beyond
will so forget themselves into
as to make this most real, most ravishing of lands
a dream
found and forgotten

14

a farunder somewhere
miraged into the hidden mind
of the lost race of dwellers and growers
diluted and adrift in an arid sea of wanderers.

WHAT NATIVES OF

dead places
know
wide
spaces

sans
noons and
tides

blanked
birdless names
calls wounded
all calling
unwoven

trees
timbered down like
weed, weeds
grief
grove

o

and
and and
hills
harrowed

amenable canyons bound
and

sweet mouths their
shadowed swales
staked
for sun slaught

the vole zones the
voteless mouse bones the quail
cast out

for
steel and stillness
for a certain
un
lived
stillness

a certain
mute
lessness
of
business

o

or
or or
galore
buy this
have havings
sooner
more

artifice of
pain
lessness

Dad shops
Mom shops
baby shops
dont ask
parents
of
shame
of
name
of

less
re
minding
if
history's a
breezy
teevee
series

amniloquent
forgetulary
deity

satiety

artifice of
pain
lessness

Hertz lot
overcovers
orchard
spot
ever oaked
before

foreoaked
forever
footplace
for mind
minding

the foremind
landing in
the mind within
bone
branch
and
being

in
the deep
grove
the memory
the slaughtered grove
and grief of
weeds

        O

assume
all perfume
purchased

no knowing
morning
leafbreaking
suncrack

no
odor
of

taste of
no bone
or stone
of

natives of
dead places
know to
not ask

what long past
love
bred places
into blood

or what
lessness
bled
loved places
dead

o

numbed
members
slumber

lest lopped

limbs
re
member
let
lessness be
kept fed
and rested

let hot be
fashion

let ad on ad
make no
sum

let round
time split
digitals
off
our hands

let no
earth drum
no sky
glow
come

no ever rain
nor bursting
sun

let here be
no place of
be

no place of
longing

let
here be
curb
numb
er

for what
dead places
tell
hails
hell

so what

natives of
dead places
know
is

no
what

NO PATH OF MY NOT MAKING

I

No path
of my not making
would I walk

for I was stronger than I needed to be
till I grew weak with the doing.

Distillment of pain
sweated into a stoppered rage
where it bit like acid at each swig
stinging long nights into aggression of study
love of truth my finest weapon
and I its only wielder.

I was stronger than I needed to be
though growing weak with the winning
and no path
of my not making
would I walk.

II

On the sweet back slope of the ridge I was laboring
or someone was.

These were my tools:
        one shovel, my own, not much worn
        one old ax, my father's
        one long-bladed trimmer to snip back
           on what trail I had made last year

and one fine lopper, double hinged
    and of a secret levering power
    that made me meditative and hopeful
    that made me laugh when I used it.

I was pushing new trail along hillside.
Above me bright ridgetop ran spiny with yucca
and dark down below was a running stream
but here, halfway, was a thicket
a fine thicket twice my height
and I was working for a good path through.

Sheer ceanothus built regions of thorn
preparing its thousand flowering.
White-limbed sugarbush knotted and tangled
though soft of wood and easily cut.
Where there was clearing, small herbs and sage.
Where there was north slope, oak.
And all places, greasewood and sumac
and the sliding hillside, and the too steep,
and the finding way, at every step.

There is a way of swinging an ax
that travels from ground
through feet and legs
and out into arms circling free
until axhead
                    buries
in earthrooted trunk.
This is the place I was laboring in.

Funny how little was thought.
I had worried over it,
imagined surveying from a top somewhere
to lay in the right way, the way above reproach,
manly, full of foresight and planning

yet in the making, as my arms clipped and cut
and the shovel came out for a couple of fast licks
the trail seemed not to be a question at all.
Always an opening.
A deer run, probably.
Or were there people here before?
Everything so overgrown.

Yet
there it is
as the bushes fall into my hands
and I into their spines and branches
as the cutters cut and the deep-hidden slopes traverse
there it is.

I smiled
thinking how this would never be
the my-trail I had sought.

Maybe
no one makes a trail, I thought.
Not really.

And then I went back to chopping and pushing.

III

That was a morning. Then a day.
Later I came back pushed or drawn
by thirty-five years of fear and old habit
and the not-my-trail I still wanted
threading the thicket
like a murmur of laughter

till finally
I sat on a rock on the ridge of Briggs Canyon
at the edge of the brink of the trail
to rest.

All breeze ceased
                        and
all the land of pools and shingles below me
            seemed to grow silent
                        and
even the world of birdsong fell away
            like a husk
            like a wrapping woven
            of all desires all beauty
            every right and comely thing
            every misshapen suburb and evil and ambition

                        and
my clothes were filthy with sweat and swale
yet from them shook out into the stillness
            a sweet odor of sage and yerba santa
            crushed in my passing
            a sweet odor
rising straight from my person
into the smoggy vault of the blue actual
and me with it
    me with it

rising as if from my old life
into one still older.

IV

It came to me then
how once along the Kern
where sagebrush and piñon grow high
then divide the land with
fir and long-needled pine
along the clefts of streams

how I had walked there
explorer of hard solitude
discovering the good site for camp
the way to walk upstream
the place to sit shaded and safe
and regard the sweep of valley

and how not even the dead hawk on the meadow
whose feathers winked the windy sun at me
from a mile off
had given me the clue

and how
hollow with silence
on the last day I lifted my load
to leave

and only then discovered
obsidian chips in a glittering city
inhabiting the sand at my feet
spread out in flakes and workings
and gathered there, by the flat rock
mortar-holed
and by that boulder
fire-scarred
and next to the slaughterbones
and sage.

Half-arrowheads, blunders, middens
then a whole one
held in my hand: tiny
but perfect
for rabbit, perhaps
or made for a child

the child at least a century away
waking briefly in the hillscape
walking by me in my other mind
held in the weight of a small hewn stone.

Paces away had been my camp
and a stream with no path seen
places of old use
which I had borrowed to invent again.
How the blood and hawk feathers
in my hatband
laughed!
And how the devil had I walked
as if by map
to this very place?
It had felt right to me
as it had to them
the trail had flowed from the land
and from my mind.

Maybe no one makes a trail
not really.

V

And on the white rock on the edge
between the city and the hill
watching how the works of man
held steady just a moment before dissolving
feeling how the brushland at my back
was never steady even a moment
but resolving always
into something else resolving

it came to me then also
how all the years of my struggle
were neither started nor finished
and all the peace I had won and demanded and
invented
had been common
and how all the blood I had drawn of myself for purity
          and of others for rage and expiation
and all the knowledge I had worked for and read
books for
and all the wisdom I had wept for not having

had been obvious
and often discovered
and had been waiting for my passage

not hidden   not open
not absent   nor present
never won   never lost
never moot never trivial never heroic

but of a value absolute like water
to be drunk, and rediscovered, and drunk again
running from the holding hands

down to the elbows and
splashing a little on the face running
from forehead and cheeks
down to the tips of the beard
into the moment of complete sufficiency
with nothing to be saved for later.

And that is when the licoricy smell of yerba santa
mixed with the herb of sage
crushed into scratches
on my face and forearms
and starting already to heal there and on the trail as
well
shook me out from my old life
into one still older

one laid into the slope of my mind
by some far passing long ago
some passing redolent of labor and hard learning
long ago.

Then
noting how the shifting winds
carried the perfume in all directions
and how exhaust and noise drifted up
and mixed with the wheel of hawk keening overhead
I rose
and rubbed my neck
and went on with my life.

VI

the
no path
of my not making
will I walk

the plain place
where everybody lives
and nothing is rhetorical or unusual

until the warm earth
shakes a bit
or the friendly hill
sends down a little magma
and the usual
is reconsidered

how the leaves of other days
are mixed casually with blood

so
I will walk the
no path
of my not making

finding the bright place
where for love of knowledge the heart
leans up against the real
letting it support the weight

and
finding the blood place
where the mind is dark

on the
no path

the past escapes me
and tomorrow slips free
from the grid calendar cage

flickers briefly
wild
glimpsed through trees

so I will walk
thinking like someone
who comes before
or after

on
the
no path
of my
not
making

II. KERN

KERN

There is a woman
who makes a meal
of acorns

There is an old woman
whose job is to keep the River
Kern

It is not a hard job
It has held many
before her

But she now
is the one who washes and pounds
and pounds again
and washes eight times again

She is breaking and sending
the tannins
She is making the fine grainy meal

She pounds, pounds
sitting straight-legged right on the ground
pounding, pounding still

It is her job
to do things
over and over
to do things
over and over again

o   o   o

She may have to live somewhere
out on the western slope
May not have seen or tasted her river
in many years

No matter
Her milky eyes see clear
And her hands run true

through piñon pine and
spiny oak leaf tangle
many-branched like memory

o   o   o

The pounding-stone she holds
a hand pounder
long-holden and old

And pounding-place, wide flat
of samestone, holed just so, so
acorns rolled, pounded, scooped so

Over the warm earth
this small burrow
opened and fed over and over
golden oak marrow

o   o   o

Her Kern is no burden
learned from before-comers
never long from the river

the long-lived-along river
the one length unturned
of river almost bendless

from snows
delivering
straight along the landbreak

into the middle lands
of the southern mountains
before the great westward sweep

There they lived, Kernwise
burning the pine and sage for incense
learning and learning the ways

o   o   o

She is making the meal

She may know, now, a few
of the old words, saved from the
flood-wreck of change

She never thinks of blame
She sometimes mumbles
an old long-syllabled name

Trouble is no news
The fish tremble
in cold waters coming alive with mayfly

and pure gravel gathers
in spawning shallows

She pounds the acorn meal

The coyote cocks his snout beside the rapid
quickening to the current
then drinks

The light of day
courses down the long rock-channeled pathway
to evening, like a very young girl or woman

who brings her woven basket down for water
each day at the time of the same time
walking with knowledgeable feet and well-combed hair

dreaming and drawing
from the same
still rushing stream

o   o   o

The acorn kernel is no big secret
It is fat with food
for a little work

So she goes on reaching and stooping
finding and spraddling out and pounding
And she has no magic but this
which is plenty

It is her job
to do things over and over
to do things
over and over again

It may be this sets her heart free
to sing and dance, if it likes
or to think, or just to get sleepy and nap
Why not?

40

o   o   o

There is silt in the many other holes
and only she is pounding
Dirt is washing down now

and only she is keeping
the one place clean
and only she is singing now

Only she is singing now
songs that tumble into the soft lap
spread to catch and cache the daily meal

And only she is singing now
while the Kern courses down, for now
from the clean tall peaks
at the top of the lap of her land

MONACHE MOUNTAIN

If there were a place where a high sage plain
    swept from the higher peaks and places
    down to a river
And if the river carried gold and snowmelt
    from left to right, left to right
    as if proving something
    to the conelike mountain on the other side
And if the cone mountain bore a name corrupted
    from people no longer standing on the banks
    which are not there, but have slid away
    and slid away, with the names of all things else

Then the people are not there still
    they are not there still

                              and they are the people

And I shall go to visit them
    corruption sliding in and out of my lungs like lies
    and the name of their mountain which I speak,
        over and over
    a black smooth stone tumbling in the river
    which I grasp out in the hand of my mouth to warm
And feel how the darkness of its weight holds me,
        just a little
    sinking or slowing just a little into weight
    weight of place and belonging

With the people on the banks not there
    and still

NIGHT SONG ALONG THE KERN

Wise are the wild stars
roaming there among
the blazing pastures far,
far, and wilderness they are.

Great trees gather on the ridge
beneath the gazing sky
balanced on a darkened edge
and in the silence
they themselves they are.

River black and full of light
banked like embers cliff to flank
yet sliding, sliding always in its heart
relentless, wavering and still
river voices, river night.

Wild is the watcher of wise stars
mindful on the silent bar
below mild breathing pines
and wilderness they are

and wilderness they are.

III. MOUNTAIN

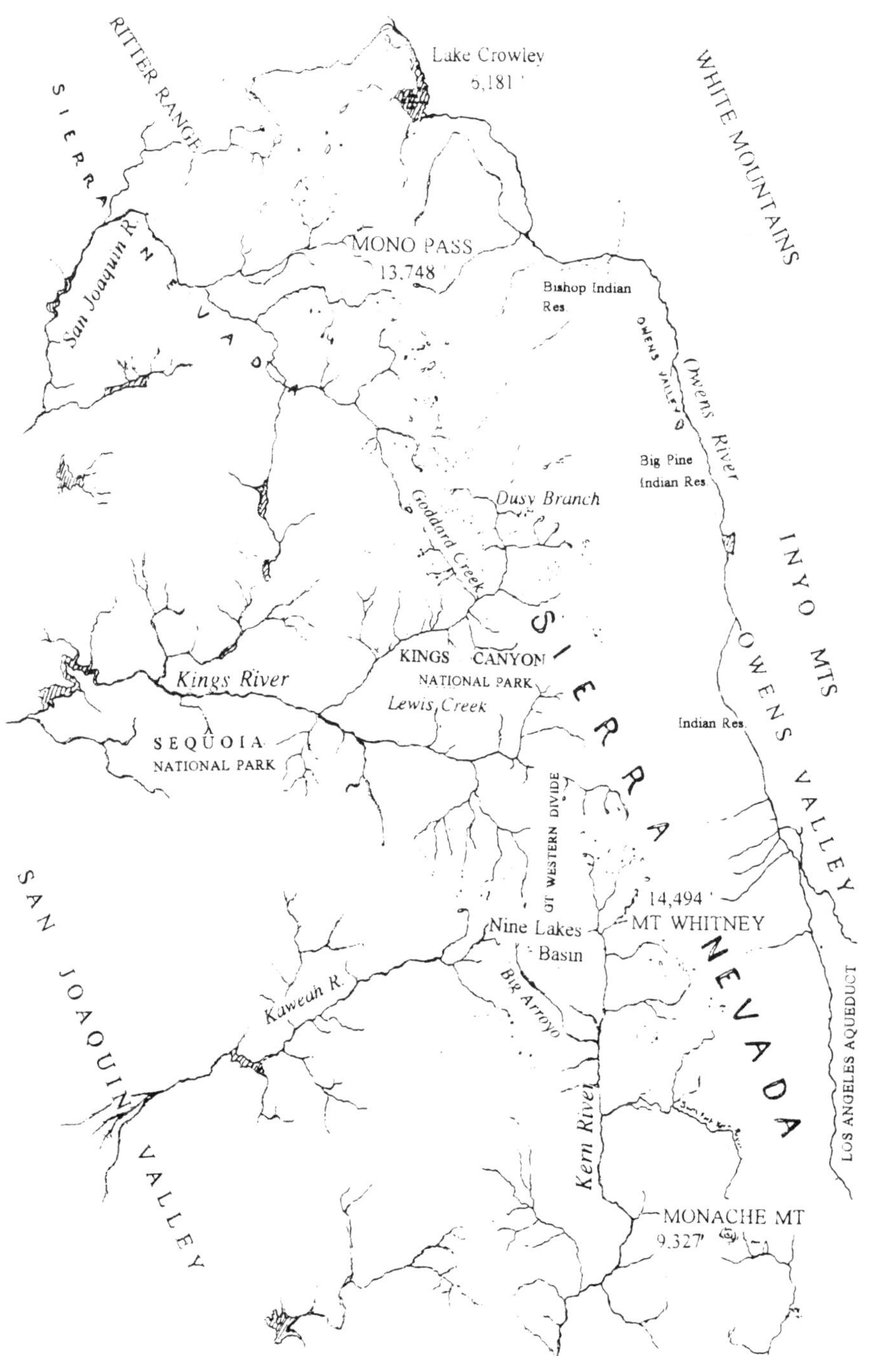

SIERRA
RITTER RANGE
WHITE MOUNTAINS
Lake Crowley
5,181'
San Joaquin R.
NEVADA
MONO PASS
13,748'
Bishop Indian
Res.
OWENS VALLEY
Owens River
Big Pine
Indian Res.
INYO MTS
Dusy Branch
Goddard Creek
OWENS VALLEY
KINGS CANYON
NATIONAL PARK
SIERRA
Kings River
Lewis Creek
Indian Res.
SEQUOIA
NATIONAL PARK
GT WESTERN DIVIDE
SAN JOAQUIN
NEVADA
14,494'
MT WHITNEY
Nine Lakes
Basin
Kaweah R.
Big Arroyo
LOS ANGELES AQUEDUCT
Kern River
VALLEY
MONACHE MT
9,327'

FIRST LIGHT

first light
early trail

now, maybe, the hominid
comes

lulled awake
by
walking

slow now
perhaps,
opens

knows, somehow
this strange

old

home

BELOW NINE-LAKE BASIN, LATE SUMMER

here

you think you can feel the
world turn

       white
       the rocks bleach through grasses
       stonesides
       rise, rise

       beyond

sitting
a hikeless, planless day
two miles or so in altitude
above the Fresno plains
two days or so from homebeds

feeling the grass-juice seep
through my pants seat
while the world spins

o o o

why do we go
to where we seem to be nothing
to grope for answers?

this beauty
what is
shedding its garments of flesh
sidereal cliffs
too large for knowing

tent of the world
pitched beneath blackness
not for shelter
just the cooled granite of necessity

o   o   o

    copse
    battered hemlocks
    rugged tufts of grass
    with, even,
    flowers

that is all

much

o   o   o

free water
purging down the marrow-course
ancient glacier track

rock of the world
under my feet

light of the distant galaxy
in my hair, my skin

sometimes the little galaxy-light
touches
green cells
    hemlock needle
    grass blade
    corn-leaf
into life-doing

and then is surrounded by
grasshoppers munching
apples of starlight

                    o   o   o

not answers

not questions

only the world
being the world
    being the
        world
        being

JUST BEFORE MOONSET, TIMBERLINE

waterfall
in the night
rushes, rushes
stays

the sleeper, not far off,
wakes to listen:

moonsilver
starsilver
granite
water

around
in slant-shadow
unmade stones
lie silent
and untouched
each in a perfect hollow
of the close grasses

the sleeper sits stonelike
back to the westering moon
reasonless
real

he will take no photographs

even to describe it
seems a falling away

STONE-CROP

boulder-slope:
yester rain running off
down the Dusy Branch
to become the Kings

here it's mostly bare-back rock
wide sheets of stream, shining
        granite, short grasses
a new place
still fresh from the ice

half a half a million years from now - ?
earth deep and silent beneath a hundred feet of forest
earth-worm wiggle down below
shrew snout, mole paddle
hoof and pad up top, and above those the rooted trees
strange the uses of carbon

stone-crop:
beside me where I rest
very small succulent
no thorn, no husk
prefers boulder-cracks for
putting down its root-hairs, up its red pudgy leaves

moist factory
making air making earth
chewing and gathering
the mica, the feldspar
making more stone-crop
making everything it can
into the image of stone-crop

who'd ever believe what's going on here

granite and sunlight
waking up
slow

THE BLACK ROCKS AT THE TOP OF MONO PASS

eyes opened to stars

love of motion
pried open cold's bite
forced the warm tongues of his legs
through stiff-shut pants
push-packed the gear
left

       though the place spoke its name
       through alders
       in rounded words with hushes between
       like the river stones

pack creaks
knuckles blue
straps wound that place beside the neck
a kind of heat
his eyes ride a slow ferry
the dim trees drift past, no birds yet
the dark ridge ahead changes
like a woman or a man
turning slightly in bed

up along the top
sun declares the tips of twelve pines
he works his own sun up quicker
gold flowing toward the hands, knees
he crashes on for a while, taking the broken trail like hurdles
slicing his lungs with skims of air
crushing gravity at every step

then
he has fully turned the one in bed
and stops to look ahead from flank
two more to go

> there is no reason for all this
> the world could be flat
> people could be intellectual mats
> of algae
> there could be no hearts
> no sunrise of blood

gravity, downhill concussions, then
climbing again, and off the next top he falls
into the valley between
he breakfasts, happy:
only the last to go

the barrier reef of this range looming
he with scuba tanks running thin
and lightheaded
starts up

the sun has still not found this side
it shocks him
he bears his load, faithful
thoughtless
climbing

then
between these peaks, the pass
spreads out an unexpected country of sand
the horizontal sun cannot quite understand this:

long, pliant shadows cast individual stones
to sunward
apart, scattered, the stones
big as dogs, as boxes
big as distant people on the plain
hard-edged like a dream of Catalonian widows
waiting

his heart is beating wildly
sand shrouds his boot tops
the black stones beat so slowly
they cannot hear

       he watches them not move
       not hear

he tries to move
moves

a mile down, another mile down
all the blood that is in him
runs him down the trail
like liquid
he cannot understand what he left there
he rummages the pack:
all sound, all tidy
nevertheless

       here another alder stream
       pauses, rushes
       though river-cold
       so round and warm
       speaking through hushes

BOB HENSLEY

Bob Hensley
(hiked the Sierra
decades
before I did)
takes a full minute
                balancing
        struggling
just to sit down

speaks in Meeting
his voice
a carton of rough stones
the one smooth one
hidden

ahead of him
                the steep switchbacks
                                and he's tired,

tired

but he won't give up
not until the

very

top

THE ODD FEAST

The odd feast
occurred in
rustling three-mil plastic wormbeings
end to end between the trees
as if in alien congress
in a Jeff pine meadow
with your backpack sprawled
and mine trussed up neatly
at opposite extremes
with Sierran softwoods smoldering in a drizzle
fetching smoke into the dripping trees and gone
while inside the long long beast

I am delicately sampling the freeze-dried applesauce
which I find sincere, with overtones of tuna.
You parse the sixteen crackers
accented with our mutual dregs of peanut paté
and with a flourish, offer.
We stink from every fold and pore.
This makes us brothers, despite everything
as does the mottling dust of three weeks' trail
insinuated up the calves from boot-sock-line to knee
at least, despite the serviceable pants
despite the days upon the cleanly boulders
hopping edge to flat until the broken fenders
of these busting mountainslags are bettered
and the steeper talus-toppling has been run
and then the rising sides and peaks of this or that — all
as free as dust and thinking as need be —
and then you on your route and I on mine the
whole last week until I find
your tent here in this clearing,

and you in it asleep,
and I exhausted at last
from travelling too light too many days,
ready for comfort in anything
anything edible
any grunt or good humor
over hazards left unexpressed.

All I had was orts of goober
and, of course, the prized applesauce.
You dumped out your pack straightway
and started cooking,
dividing with me as if with your own body
all that glamorous soup
those broken crackers
your chili-mac
and figbars of the gods.

You and your wife and bible live now
somewhere in Pasadena.
I know better than to look you up.
Sore it is and seldom
even like minds salve or tend:
no reason now, so long after,
to stop that ridiculous feasting
where odd & odd come even for a moment,
where something in the heart permits me still
to rest
and to be fed
and to be friend.

THIRD INFINITY

the blue ball
of my childhood
rolls toward something desired
and lost
now I reconsider
and decide that all is gained
and again, that I do not know yet

the vivid trout
flipping on the willow bank
the steely sky
my age: late thirties
a former lover fishes upstream
he denies it

yet I am whole
and we will eat this for lunch
over coals, somewhat charred
weather blowing in at last across the lake

and no savior here to guide us
in the cold rain
faces wet
the rinds of fish in droplets
off the pines

his hands are rough and stubby
they never loved me back
but friendship has given them a grammar
he hands over the last one
knuckles wet, red
his face placid or even happy
under the nylon cowl

which his curly beard scrapes

the forest swells around us like tympani
we are two humans netted
if we fish again next year
the blue waters may roll
some other color we cannot name

TROUT

He puts his head upstream:
something clear and indivisible requires
trout mouth — the rough tongue, the scarlet gills.

I do not fish; I plan six ways to succeed.
I return cleverly to my division and class.
I struggle to know. I find out my adversaries

and possess them. I master my profession.
I beat the system. I know the score.
I will be happy. I advance.

He puts his head upstream:
something clear and undevised requires
the smooth back, the silver crimson gold, the leap.

Trout is a way the stream has
of doing itself. Each breathes the other;
and the trout, moving,

knows nothing of water.

STARSET AND SULPHUR

All the winter that year before I knew you
I longed to see Canopus, of all things.
Furthest of all the star cities in my mind
large and brilliant in the void
whispering through the cosmos to seekers, finders
I never saw it yet.
But I saw myself searching out the highest place
the perfect air. Over mind rills I trekked
nightly, and imagined that hilltop
from which all is clear.

That summer I almost knew you
I wandered the mountains, content and searching.
My strange goals, clean and unreachable
I hummed them along trails and talus slopes
as if simpleminded. A flower.
A bird.
A blue flower beyond description blue
a bird of the dark forest and gladelight
whose cascading song I never heard.

I wonder who you are
and why, almost
I have come to know you.

Deep in the southern haze Canopus sets
shouldering purely through the murk of horizons.
If I lift my hand, it would touch you now
through the dense and sulphurous air
you nearer in the dimness than the flickering star
the fading flower
you reaching, soundless
over the strains of invisible songs.

POEM AT THE HEAD OF LEWIS CREEK

This day have I made myself small.

Caution has made me do this
fatigue
betrayal of flesh.

Another day I will visit fiercely
stone-tumbled tops of tall ranges
the places of conversion
the turning of up and down
earth and sky.

Another day I will ascend
like the deer stag I saw
traversing to summer pasture
animate and hot among the bare rocks
shoulder-height with a shining hawk.

It will be silent in first light
when I leave the soft woods.
I will pass by the herd-people
sleep-bound in their flocks like sheep.
When they roll and grow hot in morning sun
I will be turning the earth
with my strides beneath me
slogging through thin air
up beyond trail where talus flows
from slow fountains of fracturing domes and spires

until the hoop of the holy world
rings me around
and I am its center
a straight pole pointing upward
listening for voices in the wind.

This I will do another time
after the summer's first trip like an old man
after the second like one neither old nor young
then it awaits me.

And I too must wait.

A DENIAL: PROLEPTIC NOSTALGIA

Someday people will look back and envy my life.
How lucky he was to have walked woods.
To have seen live animals
big as boxcars, finned and tusked,
or even eagles, cranes, and wildcats.
How lucky he was
to live before
they will say.

Before the great dyings
before the war
before the extinctions
before the deserts grew like despair across the
continents
before laughter was swallowed up.

Though accusation may temper their nostalgia
that, after all, I might have done more. . .
I bask in their coveting.
Let them find their own Eden.

Anglo of Anglos, man of men,
rich of rich
whole and unwounded
I do not regret a thing
not a thing
I am more grateful than Solomon in his harem
dandling a plump virgin
and praising Yahweh.

I refuse to miss my own tomorrows
like the stupid old, their youth.
These trees and streams are mine.
They are not desert yet.
Let those who come after

curse.

CONSIDERED IN THE WHITE MOUNTAINS
ABOVE THE OWENS VALLEY

If you want money, why that's what you'll have.
Hold down hard. Harness. Plod.
A decade or two should do it.

If you want slate rock and piñon
          silvered by moonlight
          in the hour of stillness after the evening winds
          high on the edge of a wild useless waste
     with all the world unrolled at your feet like a scroll
     and all its mystery written
          in far escarpments, towering up clouds
          night gestures of solitary pines
          brightness of duff at your feet
     and the key to its language just one thought
     always that one thought away

Why then you shall have that, instead.

The moon goes down
clouds tumble off northwards
sleep comes.

Only the bank account endures.

POLE
        (SKY

pole
                              (sky

    moni
                             p
    um
                                  ilot)

, he said
(between ice granite upon the arête)

tasting the spherical blue word petals
and feathery frondleaves
basal   rosette   luculently downed

at the very limit of eyesight
delicately.

So the faint scent, the experience too real,
too fine to name: like

(panting, fingers and cheeks cold bitten warm,
boots frozen, cleating the gravel ledge firmly)

the sky that darkens beyond breathing
    bluesomething, black
                    (?edges in eyeglance, dizzy
        without-limit-
                blue
                    how can so flower this think so far(?
                past known color
                        blue

ON GODDARD CREEK

I

Like the trend of river always bending into banks,
or whatever draws these trout to strike
or veer away, unknowing their own reasons,

or like the place in my right shoulder
I cannot cast clear through
but must stop, or catch pain, or work around,

my nature becomes clear to me, and its limits.
Striving, it will go this far, this way;
loving, so; mistakes or laughter, thus. My bent.

I will swerve
to my own orbit eventually
no matter which way I throw myself.

I knew a man of forty, once,
who simply said, "I'm tired of being me."
Then, I thought it very strange.

II

I know no one, am unconnected in the world.
My words travel a few feet
and drop to the ground.

More than any other choosing
this has shaped and curbed me:
I have been, always, my own teacher.

Though provided with fathers aplenty
I used and left them all. The kind ones
knew kindness only. The smart were joyless.

I never found one strong enough to serve
though perhaps my skill
lay in making sure to be stronger than.

Yet it makes me grieve, and bitterly,
that I have had to teach myself so late
to know willow and pine, river and meter,

love, forgiveness, and nearly all else
like a man on a lonely planet
ciphering books in a foreign tongue.

Oh I have cherished each finding!
Every morsel has cheered me utterly,
and does so still, I cannot help it —

each needle and stone, each crook and crab of things
pieced with ache and long looking
into its place in the beautiful whole.

Yet the blanks within me
gaze out at the blanks of the world.
The shadows grow longer than what stands in light.

I cannot forgive so great an unknowing,
nor the deep gulf of my privacy
that foolish hermitage,

nor the witless gums of my teachers
mumbling in haze of evasion
while the real world, outside, called and called.

III

I listened. That is my only defense,
my joy, my food and drink,
my cold water alone under the pines:

what called was real, was beautiful,
and I could not wait to follow.
I went.

This week I labored
far into the mountains, the dear mountains.
They do not disappoint.

I have six trout — all fit into one pan,
so bragging is not my fault —
I will cook them for lunch

beside a stream four days from traffic.
I walked here without a trail
naming the birds, the plants as I came,

naming, when I got here,
the very life of rock, the crystalled granite
beside flow-banded rhyolites and basalts,

some scoured shiny under a tide
of moving ice, moving in an eon almost voiceless,
moving to a gravity of its own.

The creek slides over such old slicks.
The fish wink golden and gone
and I drink smells, colors,

shapes of all riverside columbines
and such slight fractioned flights
as eye and long care will catch.

What arcs I find scattered
and seek to make a circle of
almost content me, some times,

some times as these,
well provisioned, here beneath the pines,
with what the curve of luck and river brings.

And if no wise man befriend me
and tell me all
I will round words like stones

and smooth them,
bending with what weight I have
and let them fall.

SEPT. 4

snow blizzard
covering the dust of summer

worn trail
bright green mule-apples
first wet
then going to white

flakes drop
slant
sudden in wind off the pass

hiker in first light
hopes for let-up

he walks
head bent
uptrail

he thinks
perhaps I am Buddha Sakyamuni
going up the mountain

Buddha's cloak swirls
billowing around the legs

o o o

later
he eats
in a white bowl by a lake
blown with snow

his hands are freezing
a little afraid
he looks for frostbite

he feels unequal to enlightenment
to suffering
the Buddha is far off
or very near

just like always

o   o   o

there will be no let-up

at the foot of the pass
the hiker yields

he is not sorry to go back
though he is sorry
not to be sorry

o   o   o

downhill
back to wind
he thinks with pleasure
that his legs have held up
and that there will be solitude
of a sort
in the motel room
far below

in his mind
this trail will always be filled with snow
and he going up it

IV. DESERT

CHOLLA

cholla
illuminated needle tree
veiled threat
white light in the morning and evening
vegetable lamp
show-off
tease

silky spines made for stroking
hypodermic to inoculate
the rash
the glib

the desert-appreciator

DESERT STREAM

desert stream
beneath wide sandy wash
we know not it but its sign
  haze of green
  pickling the blaze margin
  from aways off
it runs under a groove
beneath surrounding planes and levels
walking
  you see it now
not before
not after

secrecy
  but not deceit

the stream is there
the green plants draw it up
sun-straws
and release it into leaves
  spines
pores
winds

the stream is there
and someplace down aways
or up an hour's climbing
  the waters may step out from hiding
to stand a moment reflecting clouds
or to be tickled by rough tongues

the stream is there
rounding mounds of mica'd alluvium
smoothing sand-swathes in the tough baked basin
branch-rooting knucklehills into finials and fillups
down to lush gulches brimming under

but just denied to surface suns and winds
  and seers

HONEYBEES

honeybees
not knowing the word desert
wander chuckwalla wallows
cactus gulches
sandy granite crannies
bliss-humming like addled nannies
little on aimless errands

they should know better

their octagonal vault walls are empty
their honey is fools gold
dripping on the hot day
into tiny nourishing mirages

someone should tell them
and break this old old illusion:

neither they
nor any of us
is very likely

CHOLLA TOPPER, MORNING BREEZE

cholla topper, morning breeze
trill noise, buzz, beak sizzle
feathers puffed, rustled, chest out

human walks by
nylon shushes and denim rubs
boots crunch, crunch
breath-words bloom

later
he toes coyote scats in a circle
place of the night's bayings
while out beyond seeing
faraway choppers beat up the valley
booming north

he hums, looks, walks
sits on pink granite the size of two big turtles
makes a foot noise of rubber
quartz chip or chert
the rock has just a little sound
wind rushes past its feldspar tips

but inside, the rock carries silence
like a precious egg

and
inside the fingernails and corpuscles
silence also

and
the amidst the spine-pinnacled song-wrung wren
pausing in a space without sound
notices too the other thing
the not-singing

the sitter tries to still himself
notice
the way he has seen faint stars
using the edge of eyesight
where they seep in

beneath them, the world waits
wordless as an asteroid

CANYON WREN

canyon wren
  notched in the cliff
watering his stone-sided garden
with treble rain from morning to night

he wants me to look
but he knows I can't see him

his life:

       stony bowl   holding

         sand   **bugs**
           acre   of cholla
                Joshua tree
                yucca

      a quantity of brilliant air in transit

         the rocks
         themselves
         jointed
standing high
      or
        tumbling
           off
             into gaps
       and washes

       wren-places for
       well-amplified singing

quick dashing flight

    hopping   eye-cocking

and tail-flicking

an ounce of thunderous flute-threats

     the wren sings for war
     wears herringbone for love

         moves like a traveling salesman
         nervous about his territory

     or a lonely little storybook king
     around and around his stone-sided moat

waiting

     while the big mammals
         drift
     in and out
         looking and looking for the liquid trumpet

waiting

     for another
     more interesting
     wren
     to fall
     in

NO COYOTE

coyote scat-spot
no coyote

garden-wash of cholla
windshelter
beside plants I don't know
holes and burrows I cannot enter

probably couldn't
find this place again
either

dead leaves in a warm lee

five, six grey pieces
no coyote

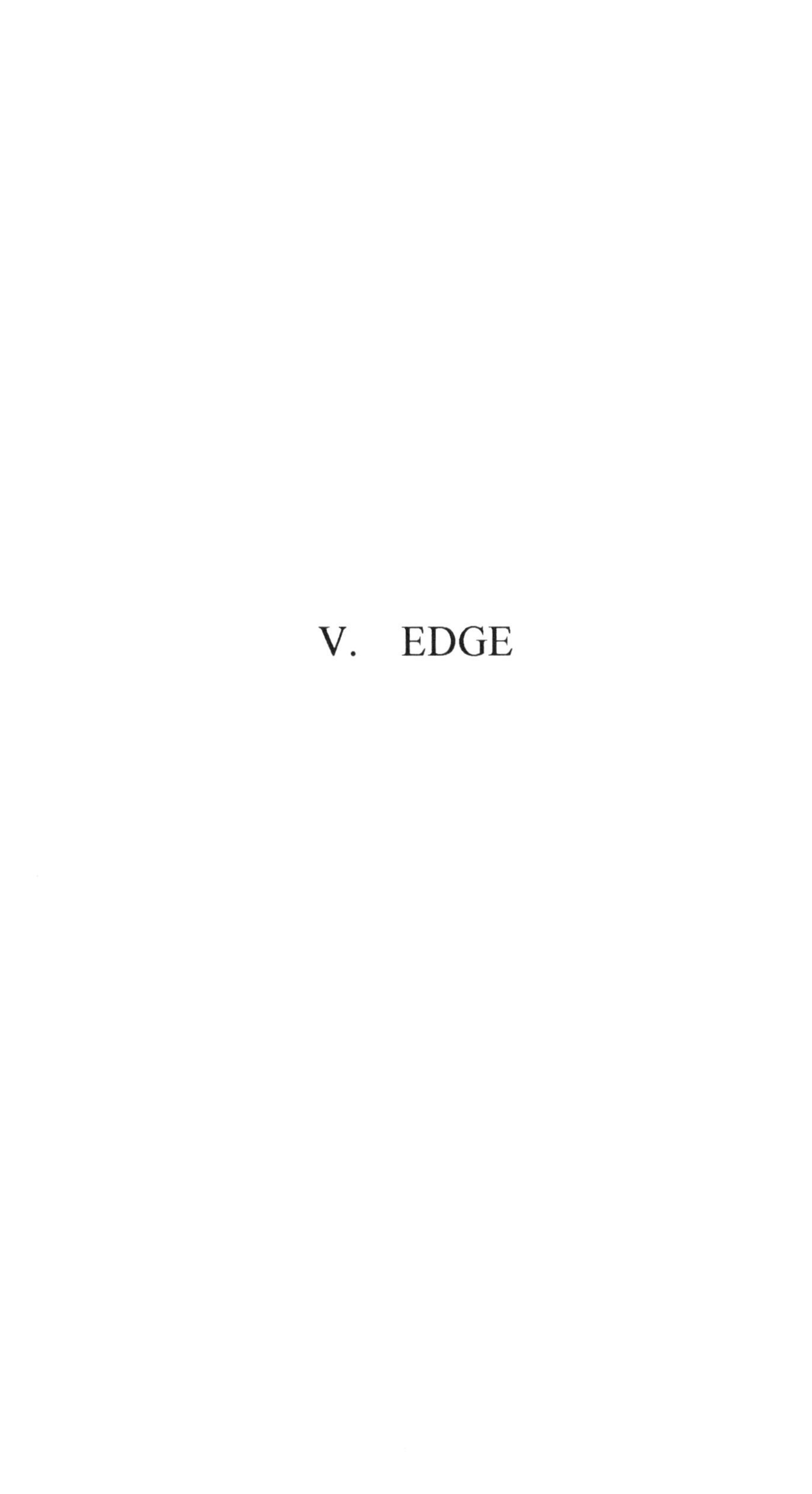

V. EDGE

WHAT THERE IS IN JOY

what there is in joy
there is also in great pain

wild the white horses come
      trampling white
         the starry surf
frothed into a cool unfathomable rage
regarding something not in you
          nor your sins
          your virtues
          your prayers
but something on a path
directly through
where you happen to be

     and their hooves will flay
and your bones crack

     and you will later heal, or not,
beneath the doubtful light of ordinary day

what darkens joy
and hides an almost joy in pain
so great this shattering
news of smallness
it seems like
almost
gain

LOOK

look
low tide
beach slick
sky and water glow
the illuminated clamshell of twilight
about to snap shut
sundown runner doesn't notice
his underman in the shiny skies beneath
soaring at just his pace
touching just sole to sole
speedy moon keeping pace to waveside
grit-spray
salt eyecorners
distant jet-black
dreamcapes

not
to rise to some sort of
fancy aesthesis
but like rough bread to take home
to eat
with no ceremony but salt
unwashed hands
hunger
then to forget
while it finds its way
into your bones

then
when you're practiced and old
will be confidence
even on neap days
lost among flotsam & smallness

(you with your stupid metal detector
sweeping & sweeping
all the while bitterly asking *Why? Why?*)
still it will be there
floating beneath your feet
the dark rich planet of reality
full of death & beauty

though
composed of nothing more than
beach grit
water smears and pools
a very large rock
the light of burnt hydrogen
and a lot of little primates
noticing

TO BE IN A GROVE

To be in a grove
of green trees
and witness the interstices
of needles and of leaves
fallen and reformed
a hundred falls and forms

within an everchanging light
that seeps through and falls or
catches and goes green
then leaches of the vivid dream
to fall through
and be fallen and through . . .

And in this light to see
light speed slowed
to stems and thorns
and wide lobed palms
that grasp a thought above a mottled ground
and web the avenues pendant down
to kernel, hip, and pome

but let it slip again,
the tilt or tip of things
not long to stem, not long to stay
but on, must on
light pouring from beyond
and pouring on again into beyond . . .

That you and I can be
that something does not stop
is but delay
and that all we know or shall attempt
is but delay
sweet, sweet delay
fondest child,
foundling child,
sweet morsel of delay.

FLORENCE BEACH, OREGON

whoever stops his running
and turns
will find death, of course

but racing before it
delight
and
many surprises

o   o   o

low bars of incoming froth
barely related to big combers further out
relax, rest a moment, return

the northward current
a southing breeze
two waves sloping back

and the one just come in
they scallop, buck
into patterns of patterns

wind-wrinkled, water-smoothed
fanlike over-
tones and exact harmonics

too many for me to follow
eye music
in endless performance

o   o   o

jelly blob
beside my footprint
beside some pink ridgy shell

soft, hard
stopped
but the beach propels past us

swifter than life
windgrain and current
relentless blessing

o   o   o

a few years back
forty sperm whales beached here and died
while far out in the world's deep water

men shot them
with exploding heads

o   o   o

my knees are grieving
over miles run
and I'm walking back

calcium, bone
fraying tendons
muscle

brainmeat
shrink-wrapped in skin
thinking pain, wave-smell, wind wrack and spectacle

here and there my stride prints
stitch toward me
one two three four nothing

o o o

up on the bluff
sandtracks spin out
behind armored cycle guys

over yielding dunes roaring
fearless to jump, fly
brocade and brodie

zig over trail over tread
until the sand forgets its grasses
and slumps into itself to wait

they are relentless, these guys
winning and showing up each other
and hollering down headlong

loading two-wheelers, three-wheelers
into the pickup at sunset
barrelling home on the freeway

bitchin dudes
ready to kill death head-on at sixty
ready for anything

but to stop
turn around
look

o   o   o

the world
moves in a mystic pace
from one moment into the next

my heart is pounding
I've climbed the dune
no one

the first stars sweep up
horizon still blue
so much we cannot destroy

this well of darkness
us things arising
the ocean stippling with light
as broad and dark as mind

the night spaces
patterned with surprise

OLD WOMAN

old woman
not frail
beside the rock-porch
shingled old house
set high away in chaparral

she checks the guy-wire
tightening the big net
of the aviary

it hums
dances
she makes a little smile
smooth and hard
like manzanita

zebra finches
canaries
flights of little birds
swirl the cage
so hard to tell frantic
from joyous

is it true the lone woman
also breeds cats
like the three in windows
behind her

she calls to them roughly
promisingly
her white hair is still full as a girl's
bright in the bitter sun

but her eyes are hooded
I cannot see them
her captives flee in circles as she moves

bird woman
cat woman
old woman
not frail

where is your husband now
and where did
his strength
go

THE DOW IS DOWN

The tao is down slightly

(this I heard distinctly
radio'd to all LA
by a distant woman)
*while stocks are mixed
and bonds are weaker.*

I could feel it, too,
as I parked off Westwood
and worked my way up among the crowd —
the well-dressed people seemed apologetic
their hands kept flashing "Well one must wear
something"
store-owners were pulling down their "Sale" signs
and the young seemed vaguely
to regret their haircuts.

Around the world
latches on briefcases were flying
tiny frantic arcs
papers describing partnerships were re-examined,
anxiously,
pre-nuptial agreements gone over yet again.
Pilots stared out at seams and welds along the wings.
People remembered their wills
or thought of what bad lovers they were.

A perceptible click had registered
and things, somehow, had gone down a notch.
Maybe we'd strayed over
some invisible line of nature.

Maybe armament researchers had laid
violent hands on something unexpectedly vital.
Perhaps sufferings in dark cells
had finally rent the fabric.
I don't know.

Each hour the radio woman will tell us
her voice silvery and arcane like some exotic alloy
how the tao is faring
and whether bonds continue to weaken.

COMFORTABLE DESERT

comfortable desert
steeliest blossom, razor-fragrant
where newspapers catch bushes
training them in politics and human nature
someday the bushes will be gone
but still newspapers will tumble in dry breezes
and people will still live here

people will still live here
heaving deep satisfied breaths of the as-if-it-were air
and will import their grandparents
who will dodder in public
and catch on fences
kleenexes will bloom in the streets
and children will ache for next year
to be exactly like this one
because this is how it is, for them,
because such traffic rumbles their golden cha-cha
because this is how it is, how it is
because you have to live somewhere

because you have to live somewhere
philosophers will emerge from P.E.
saints of astonishing gentleness rise up
          from Amway meetings
to preach to the sidewalks, the fenders, the bums
in a place like this any infamy of hope is possible
and to die here is no worse than elsewhere
god will never not speak here
just like other places
the still waters beside rut-runnels
pasture green algae in ribbons of rainbow oil

and people will find peace, or not,
down by the Fourth Street bridge
and along Riverside Drive and the Golden State
where the freeways leap playfully over rivers

where the freeways leap playfully over rivers
the fish are dead, the children held motionless
indoors by programming
the adults craven loving courageous
ignorant stupified led by
hairy politicos and dyed evangelists
into every kind of travesty and stink
every nobility and prayer
every new insight, new world of knowing
new bondage and deliverance
as the comfortable deserts of living
in all times and places
have always
never seen before

LEAN-TO

Sprained lean-to
limbs bleached spinto in the wind winter
red-rag-bound but red unraged by rain raw time

Leaning into
older childer maybe
come and gone to play

Or hobo maybe
doughboy, no boy, bye-bye

In the bushy brush
of family lands
I found it un
over top
pled
yet but sagging
still but begging
still but standing. Still

Every lean thing thins
down further, Father
or brightens down to
muffled mothers
shuffling dun
& leaning in
to winds un
seen

LOST

like a tired, tired swimmer
farthest out to sea

I can no longer tell my
strength from my weakness

that's how I know —
finally, well and truly lost

just like they always said

or maybe
my left hand pacing my right

and my lungs, like desire and duty,
filling in tandem

found
the place out there

far, far
and farther yet

where the tips of two straight lines
touch

RETURN

I want to return to my father's house
beside the stream
and live out a full sun's year, or more
though he has not finished building it himself
and the ten-month stream
hides down deep beneath sand and oak-leaf litter.

For our winter in this land
is the sullen end of summer
tapering out and out to a point of indiscernible
brilliance
and like solar bears we hibernate
dizzy in our foreheads
in the blinding cave of September
as we drive through a dream of busyness.
Around us the heat flakes drift
cars wander and hurry
kicking up thermal flurries from dazed asphalts.
Beneath them, the sand sleeps.

Somewhere within all this, we know that
October will awaken us.
The smog will lift, there will be skies
with remote strata of individual clouds
drawn across them as high
as, perhaps, the thoughts of Emerson
striding through the fields of concord.

How happy will be that simple cabin
which my father builds, unknowing
beneath the palatial trappings.
What surprise will be ours when
before the moneymaking day has broken in upon us

we arise together to follow the stream
full in its season
up the luscious cañon
drawing us higher
with the forgetfulness of leaves greening in our ears
sycamore, bigleaf maple, oaks of many kinds
and all the sweet, sharp chaparral
gathering the rugged light into thorns and burrs
mere dozens of feet above the streaming canopy
while we explore only the smooth, cool way.

There is a winter of heat in my heart for my father
and for the life of streams
and for the simple small house
abuilding.

REVISIT

The stones will be splayed with yellow lichen
bearded with long moss.
Their assertive grey, richer by mica,
will swell them to the size of refrigerators
of Chryslers, of two car barns.

On some of them I will have sat
lorded with youth.
A future infinitely long is none at all:
I inhabited my boy as I owned my
summit of stone, imperative and present.

Pines will stand around and rain
down sunlight worn down to the
drift of needles. A single jay
then none. White-whiskery fungus quiet under feet
will work an acrid mulch of what it can.

I will not attempt the sitting there.
I fear I might pass through, my atoms mingling
with the stone's, and struggle there in the thick
evanescent nature of things to climb up
to a crosslegged throne of now
with all the world obeisant and around.

THOUSAND FATHERS

Thousand Fathers sits on his heels
like this

silky skin : leg-cords cabled
underneath

he wonders what I am doing
quickens, questions

not silent : not thinking of speech :
regarding

my almost inhuman awkwardness
my shoes

o   o   o

among comfort heaped like slack rope
I sleep

and rise to talk, talk like many women
negotiating wash

all my honor is craved from employers
and paid off

neither darkness nor hunger
in this night : this day

o o o

his heavy brow, breath, muzzle :
will he kiss :

mahogany elbow strong and quick
stings

correction without looking
instead

he knows where death is, across yellow grasses
slightly bruised

he edges along the brainstem forest
nostrils branched

enters the conscious grove
silent

travels down to salacious water
rank and inviting

intelligent in breathing : moving :
living in place

o o o

I am so slow : if I turn back
Thousand Fathers

does not stop : if there is pain
I cannot tell

between him and where I sleep
there is no path

yet when I wake without thinking
he points

the long long path : the dust :
many feet :

the shining scar : the morning :
silence

STAY

being

sweetest prisoning
prisming

binding light
and wind

kindled instant
kind
and broken array

O Shiva, Shechinah
tarry my shattering

rend me
some other day

      o o o

way
of care
and of all caring

wounding
unwearying play

stone
stock and
breathing

scent of delight
carried on the dream
of a mortal
dismay

Shechinah, Shiva
spare my shivering

turn away

        o   o   o

of the hill
a stream
bears grit

to wear away
worshippers and temples
far below it

so that mingled ash and sand
cohabit
some lush plain
in some land further yet

and of each bulb or corm
of flesh

something will pry
delight into a
rubble

silt
stone
and bent

into
other flowers
on another hill
of grit

o   o   o

all things
tending

leaning into
some next thing
lending

all things leaving
unbinding
unbeing

O Shiva, Shechinah
only bless me my ending
with delay

o   o   o

O Shiva
Shechinah
starry beast of void

empty your savoring
of just this one day

overleap
these least and pleasing bonds
of carbon and thought

leave my delivering

stay

REMEMBERING THE WIDENESS OF THE WORLD

remembering the wideness of the world
the silvery fish escapes the net

the light-flashed green
the round unending deep

o o o

a person switches off the television
stands on the screened porch
breathing darkness

o o o

fluorescent neighbors writhe
meanwhile, meanplace
on sofas in blue rooms

tomorrow all will seek money
boredom and pain
like toxic, fashionable garments
they *simply must have*
and again each night will flee
money boredom and pain

O painlessness! Where are you!
they will hieroglyphically shout
in the subtleties of their discontented twitching

then the balm of objects
and strange foods
will soothe to a madness

and maybe tomorrow what is sought
will be found

o o o

on the porch
winds coast in from faraway seas
her eyes grow keen
small lights speed from friendly galaxies
and make port at last in her mind
opened like the night-flowers she smells
white-petalled in the earth below her

impossible to prevent or restrain
she drifts like golden pollen into her own life
remembering the wideness of the world

ALIEN

everyone in LA is moving somewhere else
but I don't think I'll bother

I'm becoming alien
right where I was born

my body stranges into
flab and frayed cabling

my parents sail
toward an unknown place

my home was bulldozed
and only an occasional Santa Ana

carries a whiff
of something I nearly remember

growing on a hillside
that no longer exists

VI. LO-KU

it's not just a lot of talk

it's not just a lot of talk
we are pretty young

who knows
what another ten thousand years of poetry
might do for us

This

this
is the round pond

poem rim around
surrounds stillness

you

are the stone

thrown

skies shatter
        splinter
           slim crescents scatter
   streak

settle
   seek
     rock down wrinkle

rest

this

is the round pond

poem rim around

surrounds

you

possum and cockroach sat down

possum and cockroach sat down
under the gingko tree

wide clouds span
forever sky   a man
who owned the gingko
came to worry

mountains melt like sugar
beneath the rain

duff glimmers

duff glimmers
downscatter:
aged pine bits, satin-grey
egg shells & seeds
ants, woodlice, termites
pinestraw galore
cones scaled, gnawed,
one unopened
three blades of grass

many lives
left here
many more
tending

the thing world merrily jing

the thing world merrily jing
ling small change
in its pockets

lepton dance
dont owe
nobody

nothin

I like it when the checks run few

I like it when the checks run few
right as the deposit slips do

a sense of balance: self-providence

to this
have our dreams of wholeness

shrunk

what the chainsaws have made clear

what
the
chainsaws
have
made
clear

everyone pretends not to know

"we don't know" they say
"oh no, how could we know?"

while
everything
else
the
chainsaws
touch
becomes
clearer

and

clearer

learning at last to bless

learning at last to bless
I bless:

all is well, and
all is well, and
everything is right where it should be

but when I've finished

everything has moved

home is always becoming strange

home is always becoming strange
but that dont mean it aint home

the body is a machine

the body is a machine
for turning matter into energy

the mind is a means
for turning energy into experience

the spirit is a way
to turn experience into ecstasy

ecstasy is the exact and present awareness
that matter, energy, & experience

are one

dim song

dim song
olive tree

words filter like dust
through the grove

his hands raised empty
before him, one teaches

the snake sheds its skin

the snake sheds its skin
& becomes

the snake
again

the live thing lives

the live thing lives
quietly

in a small space

a spider sits beneath my rose
arched over by a leaf, a twig

a partita plays in my other room: pure notes
sculpting the pure void

they make room to live
they wait
when it is time, they come out

so come the real words

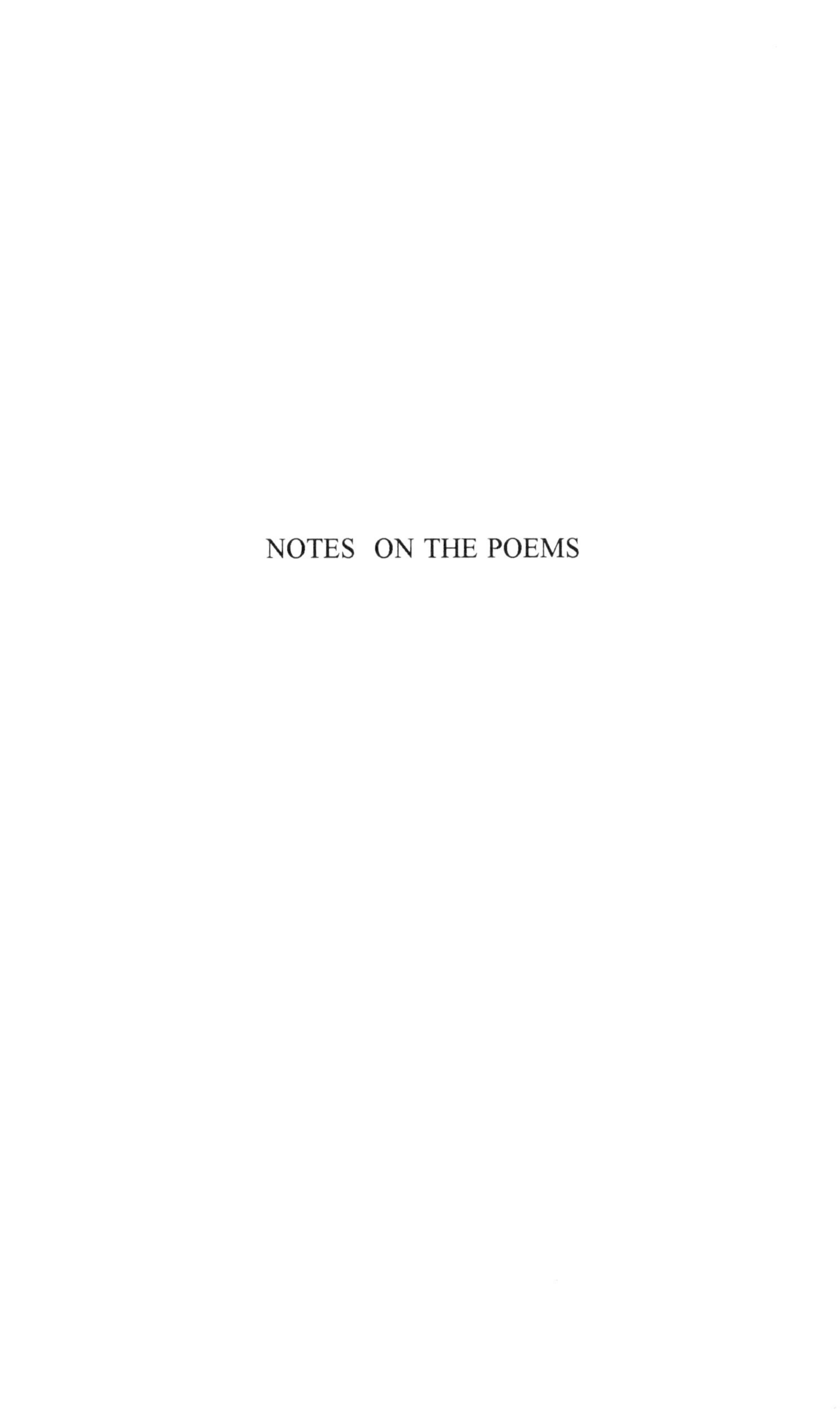

NOTES ON THE POEMS

I. CHAPARRAL

INTO THE VALLEY   (pp. 5-14)

the Valley   San Fernando Valley, a broad inland basin forming the northern part of the city of Los Angeles.

sumac   chaparral tree.

ceanothus   generalizing name for several species (genus Ceanothus) of chaparral brush. Common names for species include "buck brush" and "mountain lilac."

creosote   "creosote bush," a pungent-smelling chaparral shrub.

yerba buena   native California perennial, with strong minty scent, also called "satureja."

NO PATH OF MY NOT MAKING   (pp. 23-33)

greasewood   dominant chaparral shrub, also called "chamise."

Briggs Canyon   steep canyon in the foothills of the San Gabriel Mountains, northeast of Los Angeles.

Kern   southernmost major Sierran river, rising beneath Mt. Whitney and the Great Western Divide and running seventy miles due south in two branches, until turning west into the Central Valley. The people who lived here, for about a thousand years, were the Tubatulabal or "Kern River Indians." There are no known survivors.

yerba santa   common chaparral shrub with a distinctive odor and an anise or licorice taste, put to many medicinal uses by native inhabitants and pioneers.

sage   several different species of sage (genus Salvia)
                grow in these mountains. Many Native Ameri-
                can cultures burned (and still burn) sage for
                ritual purification; locally, "White Sage" was/is
                preferred.

II. KERN

KERN (pp. 37-41) See comments on the Kern River and its people
                in notes to "No path of my not making" above.

MONACHE MOUNTAIN   (p. 42)

Monache Mountain volcanic cone on the South Fork of the Kern
                River. The Monache (also known as Western
                Mono) were original inhabitants living north
                and west of the Kern, along parts of the Kings,
                Kaweah, and San Joaquin Rivers. In their own
                language they, like many other native Americans,
                called themselves simply "the people."

III.   MOUNTAIN

BELOW NINE-LAKE BASIN . . . . (p.50)

Nine-Lake Basin cirque in the southern Sierra on the Great Western
                Divide, draining into the Big Arroyo and Kern
                River.

STONE-CROP (p. 54)

Dusy Branch   tributary of the Middle Fork of the Kings River.

stone-crop   very small, succulent plants of the genus *Sedum*.

mica, feldspar   minerals common in Sierran granite.

THE BLACK ROCKS AT THE TOP . . . (p. 56)

Mono Pass   goes over the eastern crest of the central Sierras, just northeast of Bishop, California.

THE ODD FEAST (p. 60)

three-mil plastic   the kind used for cheap makeshift "tube tents."

Jeff pine   tall, stately Jeffrey pine, common at 6000- to 9000- foot elevation in the southern Sierra (lower in the north).

STARSET AND SULPHUR (p. 65)

Canopus   brightest star in the southern skies, visible from the northern hemisphere only at lower lattitudes or in unusually good viewing conditions; located in the constellation Argus.

talus   medium-sized broken rock on and around peaks.

POEM AT THE HEAD OF LEWIS . . . . (p. 66)

Lewis Creek   in the Monarch Divide region above Kings Canyon.

CONSIDERED IN THE WHITE MOUNTAINS, ABOVE THE OWENS VALLEY (p. 70)

White Mountains   range rising above 14,000 feet abruptly east of the Owens Valley. Across the valley to the west is the huge block-quake-faulted front of the Sierra Nevadas.

POLE(SKY   (p. 71)

Polemonium (skypilot)   flower of the phlox family; found on rocky
ridges between 10,000 and 14,200 feet in the Sierra
Nevada.

arête   narrow ridge.

basal   leaves located around the base of a plant.

ON GODDARD CREEK   (p. 72)

Goddard Creek   remote drainage in the central Sierra between the
White Divide and the Ragged Spur. It feeds into the
Middle Fork of the Kings River.

flow-banded   layered, showing evidence of molten rock in motion.

rhyolites, basalts two of the basic types of volcanic and metavolcanic
rock (contrasted with the granite which forms
most of the Sierra Nevada range.)

SEPT.4   (p. 76)

Buddha   "Buddha coming down from the mountain" is a
favorite subject of Japanese zen paintings. In the
story alluded to, Buddha ceases his fasting on
the mountain top and returns, having attained the
insight of the "middle way" — to avoid extremes
whether of asceticism or luxury.

IV.   DESERT

CANYON WREN   (p. 88)

cholla   several species of extraordinarily spiny cactus.

Joshua tree   largest yucca in the California deserts, often ten to twenty feet tall.

CHOLLA TOPPER, MORNING BREEZE (p. 86)

cholla topper   the cactus wren often chooses tops of cactus and cholla for its unlikely perch.

HONEY BEES (p. 85)

chuckwalla   large, iguana-like lizard in deserts of southwestern US.

V. EDGE

TO BE IN A GROVE (p. 95)

pome   any fleshy fruit containing a core with seeds.

LOOK (p. 97)

neap   neap tides are those having the least difference between high and low.

STAY (p. 99)

Shiva   Hindu deity of creation and destruction, often depicted with many arms, dancing.

Shechinah   Hebrew word for the "glory" or light surrounding the unnamable Yahweh. The Baptist Bible-teachers of the poet's youth Anglicized this word as "Shuh-KI-nah" (rhymes with "Dinah").

LEAN-TO (p. 113)

spinto   style of soprano or tenor singing in which the voice
is forced toward an extreme.

VI. LO-KU

IT'S NOT JUST A LOT TALK (p. 129)

ten thousand years   time since the Neolithic Revolution, i.e. the
beginning of agriculture and "civilization."

DUFF GLIMMERS (p. 132)

duff   natural forest litter becoming humus: twigs, pine
needles, etc.

THE THING WORLD MERRILY JING (p. 133)

lepton   sub-atomic particle.

THE LIVE THING LIVES (p. 138)

partita   musical suite, especially Bach's unaccompanied
violin works.